DATE DUE

MR 22 '04		
AP 04 '04		
DE 28 '05		
SE 11 '06		
MY 30 '07		
FE 14 '12		
MR 31 '12		

DEMCO 38-297

The Manx:
The Cat with No Tail

Jennifer Quasha

The Rosen Publishing Group's
PowerKids Press™
New York

Published in 2000 by The Rosen Publishing Group, Inc.
29 East 21st Street, New York, NY 10010

First Edition

Book Design: Michael de Guzman

Photo Credits: pp. 1, 8 CORBIS-Bettmann; pp. 4, 12, 15, 16, 22 © Robert Pearcy/Animals Animals; p. 7 © Robert Pearcy/Animals Animals and © Hal Kern/International Stock; p. 11 © Art Resource; p. 19 © Robert Pearcy/Animals Animals and CORBIS-Bettmann; p. 20 Gerard Lacz/Animals Animals.

Quasha, Jennifer.
    The manx: the cat with no tail / by Jennifer Quasha.
       p.   cm. — (A kid's cat library)
    Includes index.
    Summary: Relates the history of the Manx cat and describes the physical and other characteristics of this breed which came from the Isle of Man.
    ISBN 0-8239-5512-5
    1. Manx cat—Juvenile literature. [1. Manx cat. 2. Cats.] I. Title. II. Series: Quasha, Jennifer. Kid's cat library.
SF449.M36Q36 1999
636.8'22—dc21
                                                  98-53562
                                                   CIP
                                                      AC

Manufactured in the United States of America

Contents

1	The Manx Cat	5
2	The Isle of Man	6
3	Cats Aboard Ships	9
4	The Myth: How the Manx Cat Lost Its Tail	10
5	The Truth About the Manx Cat's History	13
6	Different Types of Manx Cats	14
7	The Manx Cat in Cat Shows	17
8	A Cat Fit for a King	18
9	Another Short-Tailed Cat	21
10	The Manx Throughout History	22
	Web Sites	22
	Glossary	23
	Index	24

The Manx's back is curved because its hind legs are longer than its front legs.

▼

The Manx Cat

The Manx is a special **breed** of cat that has a very short or missing tail. It is also unusual because it has long hind legs and short front legs. Since its legs are different lengths, the Manx hops instead of walks. Some people say that when it moves, it looks more like a bunny than a cat. While the Manx may be best known for its cute looks and funny hopping, Manx cats are popular pets because they are so sweet, friendly, and easy to love.

The Isle of Man

Manx cats came from an island off the coast of England called the Isle of Man. The people who live on the island are called Manx, too. Manx cats have lived on the Isle of Man for hundreds of years.

The Manx cat is so well loved by the people on the Isle of Man that in 1971, the government put a picture of the Manx cat on one of the island's coins. The Manx cat is also on one of its stamps. The Manx people are very proud of their island's cat.

The coin that has the Manx cat on one side has England's Queen Elizabeth on the other. ▶

Cats Aboard Ships

No one knows for sure how Manx cats first came to the Isle of Man. Some people believe they came with sailors on trading ships. Cats were useful on journeys overseas because they caught rats and mice that had gotten aboard. Sailors knew that if they didn't have cats with them, rats and mice would eat their food and might spread disease. It is thought that when trading ships came to the Isle of Man, some of these cats escaped and stayed on the island. These cats may have been the Manx's early relatives.

◀ *Manx cats may be related to cats that guarded ships from rats and mice.*

The Myth: How the Manx Cat Lost Its Tail

There is a popular **myth** about how the Manx lost its tail. This myth comes from the Christian story of Noah's ark. Noah knew that God was going to flood the world. Noah was trying to save the animals from drowning. Every kind of animal was on the ark except the Manx cat. Just as Noah was shutting the door to the ark, the Manx ran aboard. The Manx's tail was shut in the door and it fell off. This is the story that some people tell to explain how the Manx lost its tail.

The story of Noah shutting the Manx's tail in the door of the ark probably isn't true, but no one knows for sure how the Manx lost its tail. ▶

The Truth About the Manx Cat's History

Although no one can be certain about how the Manx developed such a short tail, scientists believe that it was because of a **genetic defect**. A genetic defect is when something in a creature's body does not develop as it normally would. Even among regular cats, sometimes a kitten is born without a tail. If a tailless cat **mates** with another cat, their kittens are more likely to be born without tails. Scientists think that tailless cats mated with other cats on the Isle of Man until almost all cats there were born with shortened or missing tails. This is probably how the Manx came about.

◀ *If two Manx cats that are completely tailless mate, their kittens may die in the mother's body. Healthy kittens are born from one tailless parent and one parent with a very short tail.*

Different Types of Manx Cats

Though having no tail is a **trait** of the Manx breed, not every Manx is without a tail. There are four different types of Manx cats. Rumpies are Manx cats with no tail at all. Risers have such a small tail that it looks like they have no tail. Stumpies have a short stump of a tail. There are even some Manx cats with long tails, called longies. Though their tails are different lengths, Manx cats' bodies are the same. Manx cats are known for their round faces and curved backs, and they all have longer legs in back than in front.

This cat is a rumpie. It has no tail at all. ▶

The Manx Cat in Cat Shows

People think the Manx cat may have existed as early as the 1500s. The breed was not well known outside of the Isle of Man, though, until the 1870s. At this time, a Manx was shown in a cat show in England. People realized how cute and unusual these cats were. The Manx cat was taken to America and was in its first show there in 1899. Only rumpies and risers can be shown in cat shows. This is because these types of Manx are the most unusual examples of the breed.

◀ *This cat is a riser. It can be shown in cat shows because its tail is so short.*

A Cat Fit for a King

The Isle of Man is so close to England that Manx cats became popular in England as well. Manx were shown in British cat shows beginning in the late 1800s. In 1901, the first Manx club was formed by Manx owners. They wanted to get together to talk about, show, and breed their Manx cats. King Edward VII, who was the king of England from 1901 to 1910, is thought to have owned Manx cats. Manx cats are known to be friendly and loyal animals. They probably made very good **companions** for Edward. Manx cats are truly cats fit for a king.

People believe that King Edward VII may have owned Manx cats. ▶

Another Short-Tailed Cat

The Manx is not the only cat with a short tail. In Japan, many families own cats called Japanese Bobtails. Like the Manx, Japanese Bobtails have longer legs in back than in front and very short tails. In Japan, Bobtails are thought to bring good luck. The Japanese Bobtail is so well loved that a temple called the Gotokuji Temple was built in the 1600s to honor the cat.

Could the Manx and the Bobtail be related? Scientists don't think so. Although the two breeds of cat look similar, the genetic defect that produced each breed is different.

◀ *The Japanese Bobtail may look like the Manx, but they are two different breeds.*

The Manx Throughout History

The unusual Manx cat with its shortened or missing tail and bunny-like hop is a well-loved cat today. Some people love the Manx so much that they think it should not be **bred** anymore. The genetic defect that gives the Manx its cute tail can also cause problems for the cat. Some kittens are born with problems in their spine or back legs. These can cause the kittens to become crippled. Healthy Manx cats, though, are a joy to own. Known for their friendliness and playful nature, the Manx is one of the best-loved cats today.

Web Sites:

http://www.cfainc.org/breeds/profiles/manx.html
http://www.breedlist.com/manx-breeders.html

Glossary

bred (BRED) When people have brought a male and female animal together so that the female can have babies.

breed (BREED) A group of animals that look very much alike and have the same kind of relatives.

companion (kum-PAN-yun) A person or animal that goes with someone else and shares in what they are doing.

genetic defect (jih-NEH-tik DEE-fekt) A problem that causes a person's or animal's body to develop differently than it normally would.

mate (MAYT) When a male and female join together to make babies.

myth (MITH) A story that people make up to explain something in their history that they don't understand.

trait (TRAYT) A feature that makes an individual special.

Index

B
bred, 22
breed, 5, 14, 17, 18, 21

C
cat shows, 17, 18
clubs, 18
companions, 18

E
Edward VII, King, 18

G
genetic defects, 13, 21, 22

I
Isle of Man, 6, 9, 13, 17, 18

J
Japanese Bobtails, 21

L
legs, 5, 14, 21, 22
longies, 14

M
mates, 13
myth, 10

R
risers, 14, 17
rumpies, 14, 17

S
scientists, 13, 21
stumpies, 14

T
traits, 14